MW00561812

50 Activities for the First Day of School

By Walton Burns

50 Activities for the First Day of School

By Walton Burns

© 2016 Walton Burns.

All rights reserved. No part of this book may be reproduced, introduced into or stored in a retrieval system, or transmitted, in any form, or by any means (electronic, mechanical, photocopying, recording, or otherwise) without the prior written permission of the copyright holder.

Published by

Alphabet Publishing
1204 Main Street #172 Branford,
Connecticut 06405   (203) 442-5222
info@alphabetpublishingbooks.com

www.alphabetpublishingbooks.com

ISBN: 978-0-9977628-1-5 paperback
        978-0-9977628-0-8 ebook

LCCN: 2016911493

Design and composition: *www.dmargulis.com*

COUNTRY OF MANUFACTURE SPECIFIED ON LAST PAGE OF BOOK

Contents

Online Resources

At www.alphabetpublishingbooks.com/first-day-of-school-resources
you can download free worksheets and templates that you can pho-
tocopy and use in your classroom.

Other Books by Alphabet Publishing

On the Board:
200 Fast, Fun & Easy Warmer, Filler and Fast-Finisher Activities

This curated, classroom-tested collection of over 200 proverbs, quotations, brain teasers, riddles, puzzles, and jokes is literally the easiest warmer activity in the world. Get students into the habit of coming into class, looking at the board, and getting to work independently.

What Teachers are Saying

"This is an excellent collection ...It also makes the start of class very good and studious."

"I plan on using them with lessons, as well as with my conversation groups. I also like how I can use many of the activities with mixed level classes."

Buy it Now

Buy at Amazon, www.alphabetpublishingbooks.com or anywhere else you buy books. Available in print or ebook

Introduction

The first day of school is not my favorite day. As a teacher, I pride myself on knowing what my students like, what kinds of activities they enjoy, and which teaching methods work best for them. But on day one, I don't know any of that about my students yet. On that first day, I am trying to get to know them. And they are trying to get to know me, as well. So they're a bit more reserved. That makes it that much harder to figure out how best to engage them. It's tempting to resort to a long introductory lecture or to go over the course syllabus in painstaking detail. Or just to dive into the material.

And yet as difficult as the first day is, it's also the only chance you have to start fresh. After the first day (or couple of days), expectations are already set for you and for your students. That first day is the time to set the tone for the course. It's a chance to tell them your rules and expectations. And to find out their expectations. Day one is also an opportunity to build rapport with your students and between them, while they are still looking for their place in the class. Something as simple as learning their names on the first day will also go a long way to making the students feel comfortable.

As a teacher who dislikes stepping into a classroom cold, I've come to rely on a set of established activities that let me take care of all that first day business, that require very little prep, and that engage most students. This book is a collection of fifty of my favorites, with clear instructions and variations where possible. For example, many of these activities are designed with beginners in mind. I've tried to indicate how those activities could also be used with more advanced English learners.

Obviously, not all of these activities are my own creation. Many of them are classic icebreakers and children's games. I am also grateful to my fellow teachers who shared their favorite first day activity ideas. While the inspiration for the activities may have come from elsewhere,

I have not shared anything here unless I have adapted or changed it sufficiently to make it my own. In all cases, I have tried to give credit to the person or source where I learned about the activity. I apologize if I have forgotten anyone.

Finally, just because these activities work well on the first day doesn't mean you can't also use them at other times. Students continue to get to know you and each other throughout the year. They have changing interests and expectations from the class. They may need a reminder of the rules in the middle of the semester. So don't limit your use of these activities to any one time of the year.

But hopefully they will help you begin your class well from the start.

Getting to Know Them

3-2-1*

This is an easy getting-to-know-you activity that can be adapted in many different ways.

1 Ask students to take out a piece of paper and write three interesting facts about themselves, two hobbies or things they like to do, and one thing they would be doing if they weren't in class.

2 Ask them to find a partner, swap information, and then report one interesting thing about their partner back to the class.

3 Alternatively, you can hang the papers on the wall, have students find an interesting one, and then form a question to ask the person who wrote it.

---

* *I learned about this activity from Shelly Terrell (*www.shellyterrell.com*).*

The Same and Different

Students find similarities and differences with a partner.

Put students in pairs and have them question one another until they find two similarities and two differences. Have them report back on the most interesting similarity or difference.

Variations

Have the pairs find five things they have in common.

Make groups of four from two pairs. The four then have to find five things in common among the four of them. Now combine the four into groups of eight and have all eight students find five things in common or as many as they can. Keep going, forming bigger groups until you have the whole class together again.

Find Someone Who...

This activity should be in every teacher's toolkit. It can be used to review or practice almost any grammar point or vocabulary set. But it's also a great way to help students get to know each other. This one does require some preparation, however.

1   Prepare a sheet of paper with two columns and as many rows as you have students. At the top of the first column, write "Find someone who..." and at the top of the second column, write "Name." In the first column write phrases that complete the sentence "Find someone who..." and that are likely to be true of at least one student in your class. For example, "has a birthday in the summer" or "can play a musical instrument." The phrases can be random. You could choose to target basic biographical information or hobbies or things people can do. You could practice a particular grammar structure or set of vocabulary too.

2   Hand one copy of the form to each student in the class. Ask them to go around the room and find one person who fits each description on the sheet. That person should sign their name, or initial.

3   Students sit down when they have found one name for each statement.

Optional Rules

Students can only write their name once on each sheet. In other words, if Rodrigo both plays guitar and has a birthday in the summer, he can only write his name in one space on each sheet.

Students cannot show their paper to each other. This makes it slightly harder to copy.

Students cannot ask questions directly. They must broach the subject naturally asking questions such as, "Do you enjoy eating?" "Do you spend time in the kitchen?" and then, "Do you like to cook?"

You can also make different versions of the sheet, so students cannot collaborate as easily.

Two Truths and a Lie

This is another classic icebreaker that is easy to do with no preparation.

1 Write three sentences on the board about yourself. Two should be true and one should be a lie. You can target the false statement to the level of your students and how well they know you. It should be plausible, but clearly false. Statements like, "I can speak six languages," when you can actually speak five are not ideal, as it's hard for students to guess a technicality. Another good strategy is to choose truths that are a bit unbelievable.

2 Ask students to guess which sentence is the lie. Encourage them to reason aloud.

3 When they have guessed, give them one to three minutes to think of two truths and one lie about themselves. You may want to go around and monitor. Discourage them from coming up with clearly false statements such as "I can fly like a bird" or contradictory statements like "My name is Michael" and "My name is Ali."

4 Put students in pairs or small groups. Have them play the game with each other.

Desert Island Choices

This is a well-known party game that makes a nice getting-to-know-you activity. It can be varied in countless ways. The ultimate goal is to get students to talk about some of their favorite things.

1 Make sure students know what a desert island is—an island without people or buildings.

2 Ask students to imagine they are going to be trapped on a desert island. They must name one book, one song, and one person they would bring with them.

3 They can discuss this in pairs or small groups or do it in front of the whole class.

Weird Attendance

I thought of this activity as a way to keep all students active while I took attendance, but it's also a great way to get students to teach you each other's names. This works best in classes where the students know each other. The idea is to get the students to tell you each other's names by using fun descriptions. Ways to do this include

- Calling on students to tell you if another student is there: "Michael, is Sarah here?" Get Michael to point out Sarah to you. Then ask Sarah to tell you about another student.

- Calling on students to tell you the names of other students you describe, such as, "What's the name of the girl wearing dark glasses?" You may need to tread carefully here, as you never know what physical descriptions will make students shy.

- Asking students open questions about the class such as, "Who's the nicest student in class?" "Who likes English the most?" "Who has the next birthday?" Let them debate and introduce each choice to you. This is a great way to get information about your students and find out their names.

Meuume*

This is a repetitive, but fun introduction game. The name of the game comes from the order in which students are supposed to say their names (me, you, you, me).

1 Put students in a circle.

2 Have student 1 go into the center of the circle and face student 2.

3 Student 1 says their name to student 2.

4 Student 2 says their name to student 1.

5 Student 1 repeats student 2's name.

6 Student 2 repeats student 1's name.

7 Student 1 moves to student 3 and they introduce themselves in the same way: Student 1 says their name, student 3 says their name, student 1 says student 3's name, and student 3 says student 1's name.

8 Student 1 steps forward to student 4 and continues in the same way until student 1 has made their way around the circle and exchanged introductions with every other student.

9 Now, have student 2 begin the routine with student 3, and then move on to student 4, 5, 6, and so on. When student 2 has talked to the whole class, student 3 begins with student 4, and so on.

Variations

The class breaks into two lines facing each other. Students do the routine to the person in front of them and then step to the right. The two people at the end of the lines join the beginnings of the other lines, thus creating a circuit.

---

* *I learned about this activity from "Icebreakers and Name Games" (2011).*

You can also make this more authentic by turning the introductions into sentences:

- Hi, I'm Dave.
- Hi, I'm Sarah.
- Nice to meet you, Sarah.
- Nice to meet you, Dave.

Ask the Teacher*

This activity plays on the curiosity students often have about their teacher. It's also really simple and provides good practice in asking basic questions, so it's good for beginners.

1 Draw a giant question mark on the board.

2 Tell students that they can ask anything about you that they want. As students ask questions, correct their question forms. Since it's day one, you can do this in a couple of ways that won't humiliate students.

   • Quietly write correct questions or chunks on the board. If a student asks, "Where you from?" write "Where are you from?" If a student asks, "What is you name?" write, "your name." If you are teaching beginners, these notes can be the beginning of your first lesson.

   • Wait until you hear a similar mistake multiple times and then address the class as a whole without singling out any one student.

   • Begin teaching finger counting as a silent correction method.

3 You may also want to focus on cultural appropriateness of questions if students ask you questions that are generally considered rude to ask a stranger in English-speaking countries.

4 Let students ask for as long as you think appropriate. Five to seven minutes is usually enough.

5 You can follow up by asking the students to answer the questions that they have asked you. If you make this the rule from the beginning, you will cut down on rude questions quickly.

---

* *This activity is adapted from a class that Jason Renshaw posted about on his wonderful but now defunct English Raven blog.*

Answers on the Board*

This is a simpler version of Ask the Teacher. You give them answers and they guess the question. Great test of their knowledge of basic information and question forms.

1   Think of a few basic questions about yourself that have simple answers. It's best to come up with a few typical small-talk questions like, "Where are you from?" or What is your favorite sport?" and a few less typical questions like, "When did you finish college?" or "What kind of car do you have?"

2   Write the answers on the board.

3   Tell the students that it is their job to make you say the answers that are on the board. They should do this by asking you questions they think the answers will match.

4   As students ask questions, answer them honestly. If they get close, you may want to give them a hint. For example, if you've written 1999, the date you graduated from university on the board and a student asks, "When did you finish high school?" you could say something like "I finished high school in 1994, and I went to university after that." Depending on the level, decide how strict you will be about their question forms.

5   Once students have guessed all your answers, they can play the game with partners, putting their answers on a piece of paper instead of a board.

---

*   *This activity is adapted from an idea I first saw on* esl.about.com.

Tell Me about Me

This activity is another one that plays on students' curiosity about their teacher. This variation works best if you have a class of students that have had you before in different classes and thus have different pieces of information about you. However, this is not an activity for the weak, as students can be brutal in their assessment of you.

1 Put a big question mark on the board.

2 Tell students that you are going to begin by asking students to say what they know about you. This might be from your appearance or what they have heard or what they think is true of teachers.

3 One at a time, let students guess things about you, correcting them when they are wrong. As necessary you can draw students' attention to things such as the presence or absence of a wedding ring, your clothes, or things you might have placed on the desk. You can also ask leading questions such as, "Do you think I am well organized or not?" and draw their attention to the way you have arranged your papers.

Allow five to seven minutes.

In a small class with brave students, you can ask students to volunteer to stand up to get the class to ask about them.

Never Have I Ever, Classroom Edition

Drinking games and party games often make good icebreakers. In class you will likely have to skip the drinking part.

1 Tell your students to name something they think many people in the class have done but they have never done themselves. Good school-friendly examples include flying in an airplane, going on summer vacation, and studying French or some other language.

2 Go around in a circle and have the students share their ideas phrased as, "Never have I ever..." [flown in an airplane]. For lower-level students you can have them say, "I have never..."

3 All the students who have done the action should raise their hands.

4 If only one student raises their hand, that student should explain the details.

5 Keep going until everyone has said their statement or every student has raised their hand.

Variation

Instead of doing this in front of the whole class, students can mingle and ask each other, "Have you ever...?" If they find a student who says yes, they should ask for details. Students can then report back to the class something interesting they learned about a classmate.

Another variation is to have students think of something they have done, but no one else in the room has ever done. They can then mingle, asking each other, "Have you ever..." Every time they find someone who has done the action, they have to share details and then think of a new action. Students can then report back something interesting they have learned about a classmate.

Sorting Line

This getting-to-know-you exercise that can be made more interesting by not letting students talk! It works best in groups of four to eight students, so break your class into groups as needed.

1 Tell students that they must get into a line by height, with the tallest person on one side and the shortest on the other.

2 Now, tell students they must line up by birthday with the people with early birthdays on the left and those with late birthdays on the right. You can let students talk or make it more challenging by not letting them talk.

3 Once they have lined up, check that they are correct by getting everyone to tell you their birthdays.

4 You can continue this by getting students to line up by alphabetical order of names, years studying English, years in the US, color of shirt (in rainbow order—red, orange, yellow, green, blue, purple), how many cups of coffee they drink in a day, or almost any quality that can be quantified.

Variation

A more complex version, which can be done at the end of the year, is to have a group of students choose a criterion and line up by it. You or the other students then have to guess the criterion.

Draw Me Out*

This is a quick and fun exercise that gets students to introduce them-selves by drawing a picture of themselves and then presenting it to the class. You can then put the pictures on the wall and have a bit of nice classroom decoration.

1   Quickly sketch yourself on the board, including your head and shoulders. Include two things distinctive about your appear-ance. Add one thing next to you, or in your hand. Remember that this is not art class, so feel free to make it a rough sketch. In fact making it too nice can intimidate your students.

2   Present yourself, explaining what features you played up and the item you included. Use the presentation to introduce your-self, modeling what you want students to do.

For example: "This is me. I drew my hair because it's always kind of messy but I really like it. In fact, I used to have really long hair, down to my chest. I also drew a serious face because people say I look serious all the time, even when I am happy. And I'm holding a book because I love to read."

3   Ask the students to get out a piece of paper (if you want to hang these on the wall, provide them with white paper). Ask stu-dents to sketch themselves and include two things about their appearance that are important as well as one item. Give them five to seven minutes.

---

*   *I got the idea for this activity from Woodward (2009).*

4   Now ask the students to present themselves including the things they wish to feature about themselves and the item. In larger classes, they can do this in pairs or small groups.

5   If you want to give practice in interviewing or verb shifts, students can work in pairs to present themselves to one another and then present their partners to the class.

6   Students can also work in pairs and draw one another and then interview one another to learn some interesting facts, which they can then present to the class. Students should explain why they drew their partner the way they did. For example, "He has big glasses, so I noticed them right away." You will want to monitor this to be sure students are showing sensitivity in the features they choose to highlight.

Where Are You From?

This is a great getting-to-know-you activity that works well with students from different countries or different parts of the country. If you have students from all over the world, you will need a world map. If you have students from all over the country, you will need a country map. Put the map up on the wall before class.

1 Hand out sticky notes or similar labels to students. If your map is on a bulletin board, you can hand out small strips of paper that students can pin to the map.

2 Tell students to write down their name on the paper and stick it to the map in the place where they are from.

3 Have the students look at where their classmates are from and then form one question they have for a fellow classmate. This should be based on where they are from and might include asking about their language, culture, or food.

4 Students then find the person they have a question for and ask it. Allow them to chat for a few minutes.

5 Students then report to the class one interesting thing they have learned.

In Your Own Words

I always do this activity in my classroom. Having a poster with the students' languages shows my interest in them as a person. It builds rapport when I try to use their language, and it also builds class rapport as students teach each other their languages.

1   Put up a piece of paper on the board with some basic phrases in English and then space for students to write. It can be a table or a word cloud. I like to use "Hello," "Thank you," "How are you?" "Goodbye," "Yes," and "No."

2   Tell students they can use the poster to share their languages. During breaks or before class, they should write the phrases in their own languages, or a language they know. It can be surprising how many languages your class knows.

3   Before starting class, take a look at the chart and note any new information. Give students a minute or two to discuss what they have added. This often leads to discussions of formality and register, as students debate different ways of greeting people in their language.

Who Wrote That?*

A simple and fun getting-to-know-you exercise that gets students talking to each other quickly.

1 Hand out one or two slips of paper to each student.

2 Ask students to write one thing about themselves that no one else in the room knows on each slip of paper.

3 Collect the papers and mix them up. Give each student one of the jumbled slips of paper.

4 Each student must now find the person who wrote the slip of paper in their hands by asking questions of each other. When they find them, they can engage them in conversation and learn more details.

Optional Rules

Students cannot show their paper to each other.

Students cannot ask questions directly. They must broach the subject naturally asking lead-up questions.

---

* *I first learned about this activity from Stephanie Owens.*

4-3-2 Intro*

This is a well-known fluency activity that can also help students forget to be reserved because they are so focused on speaking fluently.

1 Divide the students into two groups, A and B. Put them in pairs with one A and one B.

2 Tell them that the A's will start by talking about themselves for four minutes. Count down so you can time them, and then let them talk. It can be challenging to talk about yourself for four minutes, but encourage them to keep going. You can remind them of the kinds of things people talk about when they just meet.

3 Now put them in new pairs of A and B. Tell the A's that they will talk about themselves again, and they should tell the same basic information, but they only have three minutes to do it. Tell them to focus not on talking faster, but on speaking more fluently and also on focusing on important details.

4 Put them in new pairs of A and B one more time. This time give the A's two minutes. This should result in fluent speaking and concise introductions.

5 Once the A's are done, have the B's introduce themselves in the same way.

---

* *Paul Nation first came up with the 4–3-2 fluency activity.*

Class Survey*

In most getting-to-know-you activities, the student chooses what they want to say about themselves. In this activity, the class decides what it wants to know.

1 Ask students to think of something that they want to know about their classmates. This should be a survey-style question such as "What is your favorite food?" or "What languages can you speak?"

2 Have the students form a question and then go around the room asking their question to the other students in the class. Depending on your goals, you could also have students write a questionnaire with or without answer choices.

3 Once students have asked everyone in the class their question, they can compile the results and report to the class. For example, "Hamburgers are the most popular food in the class; 50% of the class like them; 20% of students say their favorite food is sandwiches; and only one person likes chicken nuggets." You can adapt your expectations to the level of your class.

---

* *This was inspired by a feature that used to be part of the Sunday Boston Globe comics for which students would survey their class, draw graphs, and send them in to the paper.*

Name Chain

This is a short and simple way to remember your students' names and get them to remember each other's names.

1 Introduce yourself. Say something like "My name is Mr. Burns" or "My name is Walton."

2 Call on a student to repeat your name and then give their own name. For example, "His name is Mr. Burns and my name is Peng."

3 Call on a third student to introduce you, the first student, and then themselves. Continue in this fashion. If the speaker forgets a name, get the student to repeat their own name.

4 As the teacher, you go last and introduce everyone in the whole class.

Memory Chain

This is a fun game that gets students learning about each other and, most importantly, teaches you their names right away. Depending on the size of the class, this one can take a bit of time.

1 Before class, make one card for every student in your class and put a number on each card, starting from 1.

2 Find the student with the number 1 and ask them to say their name and one interesting fact about themselves. Try to nip in the bud any facts that could apply to a majority of your students to prevent a lot of repetition, which is boring and counterproductive.

3 Now find student 2. Student 2 has to introduce student 1 by repeating their name and fact and then say their own name and a fact about themselves.

4 Student 3 must repeat student 1 and student 2's introductions and then introduce themselves in the same fashion. Continue in this way until all the students have gone. Then tell the students that it's only fair that you repeat all of them. This is a great way to remember names and also to show that you are listening and care about them.

5 If a speaker forgets a name or fact about a student, get that student to repeat it. The more repetition, the better everyone will remember everyone's names.

Toss a Ball*

Another simple name-learning game that adds some action to make it a little more dynamic. Be sure to use a ball that is not too hard, as not all students are good at throwing or catching. This game can also devolve into students throwing the ball as hard as they can at their buddies, so to avoid injuries I'd recommend a soft squishy ball or a bean bag of some kind.

1 Throw a ball gently to a student to catch. Ask the student to say their name.

2 Prompt that student to throw the ball (gently) to another student. When that student catches it, ask that student to say their name.

3 Continue in this way with students throwing the ball to one another and the student who catches the ball saying their name. Make sure that the ball is always thrown to a new student, so that everyone catches the ball and says their name once.

4 After a few rounds, introduce a new rule. Now, students must announce the name of the student they are throwing the ball to. If they accidentally throw the ball to the wrong student, they get a strike. Three strikes and they have to sit down.

Variations

Students can catch the ball and name the student who threw it, as well as their own name. This can be done as a mini-dialogue: "Thanks Sarah. I'm Mei."

You can have students throw the ball to the same students in the same order every round or have them throw the ball at random.

When you start having students announce whom they are throwing to, you can introduce a second (or third or fourth) ball, so students are constantly having to listen for their name.

---

* *I learned about this activity from "Icebreakers and Name Games" (2011)*

English Names

Giving students English names can help them get used to English names, set aside class as a special time, add to the immersion feel of the class, and help form a bond in the group. It should never be implied that we give students English names because their real names are hard to pronounce or don't fit in our country or anything of that nature.

There are many ways to do this:

Give them the English equivalent of their real names. For example, Pyoter or Pierre becomes Peter. The French male name Jean becomes John. Masha becomes Maria or Mary. Obviously this doesn't work for every name or every language. This might lead to a discussion of other words with the same roots in their language as in English and why that is.

Ask students to research English names on the Internet and come up with their own equivalent, either etymologically or in some other sense—though this can be quite challenging.

Let the students pick their own names. Some students may have a favorite English name.

Let them pick names of famous people they admire or respect.

Give them mascot names like Wolf, Hawk, or Cat. It could even be a flower or an object that is important to them such as a rose or a paintbrush. Let them pick a totem animal or object and explain why they chose it.

Have them come up with a name based on some characteristic. For example, my students love the fact that I play the guitar so I have sometimes used the name Guitar.

Going on a Picnic

This is an old camping game that you can use to memorize names. In the original version, students have to guess the rule you are following. This modified version helps you memorize students' names.

1 Say, for example, "I'm going on a picnic. My name is Walton, and I'm bringing a watermelon." Choose an item that begins with the same letter as your name. Explain this to students.

2 Call on a student to make a similar sentence about themselves. For example, the student could say, "My name is Ali and I'm bringing apples." If necessary, remind them that the item they are taking should begin with the same letter as their name.

3 When that student has answered, repeat your sentence and his. So you would say, "My name is Walton and I'm bringing a watermelon. His name is Ali and he's bringing apples."

4 Now call on a second student. The second student must make a sentence about themselves, such as "My name is Paula and I'm bringing plates."

5 Now ask the first student (Ali) to repeat his sentence and Paula's sentence. So he would say, "My name is Ali and I'm bringing apples. Her name is Paula and she's bringing plates."

6 Continue in this fashion with each new student introducing themselves and then the previous student introducing themselves and the new student again. The repetition helps students to memorize each other's names.

7 If you are feeling brave, at the end, you can try to repeat everyone's name and item. This helps students feel that you were listening and that you care about learning their names.

Original Guessing Game Variation

In order for you to judge whether the students are playing the game correctly, you will need to know their names. You could have students wear name tags, or you could play this later in the year to reinforce their names. Names are not mentioned directly, but in helping students understand the rule, other students will be asking each other's names quite a bit.

1   Say, "I'm going on a picnic and I'm bringing a...." Finish with the name of something that begins with the same letter as your name. For example, "I'm going on a picnic and I'm bringing a watermelon." Do not tell students this rule, however.

2   Ask a student to tell what they will bring on the picnic. If the student correctly names something that begins with the same letter as their name, praise them and call on another student.

3   If the student does not follow the rule, say, "No, you can't bring that." This gets very frustrating fast so you may need to hint that there is a rule about what they can bring. You can also give more examples for your own name. For me, it could be: a water bottle, a walking stick, waffles, or walnuts. You can also hint by telling a student something they can bring.

4   As students get it, encourage them to chime in and also help the other students until everyone gets it. You can then do this as a chant, as described above in the name-learning section, so that everyone learns everyone else's name.

Optional Rules

You can choose whether you want to limit them to items that would make sense to bring on a picnic. In fact, how useful the items the students say they are bringing can be a great source of discussion and a good laugh.

Expert Game

This gives students a chance to share what they are good at and interested in.

1 Ask students to think about something they are good at or know a lot about. It can be anything, but hopefully it's something that expresses their personality. You may want to go around the room and ask the topic and why they chose it.

2 Put them in pairs and have them tell their topic to their partner.

3 Have their partner think of three questions to ask about the topic. The questions can be related to the topic or they can be general questions such as How long have you been making websites? or Why do you like snakes?

4 Partners take turns interviewing one another. Encourage interviewers to ask follow-up questions as necessary.

5 Each pair should then tell the class (or a larger group) something new they learned about the topic.

Snowball Fight*

A variation of Who Wrote That? plus throwing things around the classroom!

1   Hand out a piece of white copy paper to each student.

2   Have each student write one interesting sentence about themselves on the paper. Get the students to crumple up their paper into a ball.

3   Tell the students to throw their papers around the classroom at the count of three. Try to discourage them from throwing them as hard as they can at each other. You can let this go on for a while or limit them to one throw.

4   After throwing, each student finds a snowball near them, opens it, reads the sentence, and tries to find the person who wrote it by asking questions of each other.

---

* *I first learned about this activity from Shannon Boss.*

Snowball Texting

In this variation of a snowball fight, students chat with each other via snowballs.

1 Hand out a piece of white copy paper to each student.

2 Have each student write one question that they would like to know about a classmate on the paper. Get the students to crumple up their paper into a ball.

3 Tell the students to throw their papers around the classroom at the count of three. Try to discourage them from throwing them as hard as they can at each other. You can let this go on for a while or limit them to one throw.

4 After throwing, each student finds a snowball near them, opens it, reads the question, and answers it.

5 Tell students to crumple the paper up again, throw it, and find a new paper.

6 Have students open that paper, read the conversation, and respond.

7 Continue this until you feel students are satisfied or set a time limit.

Optional Rules

Students must continue the conversation—no non sequiturs.

Students must add an answer and another question.

Time Capsule

This activity pays off more on the last day of class than the beginning. Students create a time capsule of things that define them now and see how they have changed by the last day of class.

1 Bring a box to school that will hold the students' contributions to the time capsule.

2 Ask students to contribute something personal or something related to their language proficiency, or both.

 Personal items would include a survey of likes, dislikes, hobbies, and regular activities. You could ask students to write their favorite color, favorite band, favorite hobby, favorite sport, one thing they are looking forward to, and one thing they want to remember forever, for example.

 Language items would include a paragraph about themselves, a grammar exercise, a proficiency test, a recording of them speaking, or a video of them doing a roleplay. You could record students interviewing one another and save the videos to a flash drive that you will save until the last day of class.

3 On the last day of class, have students repeat the task or survey they did on the first day. Then let them compare the results. If you are focusing on proficiency, have them note some of the progress they have made.

Assessing and Evaluating

Needs Evaluation Survey*

Giving students a survey to fill out is a great way to find out their needs and interests for class. There are a number of ways to do a needs evaluation. Depending on the level of the student, the tenor of the class, and their familiarity with survey instruments, surveys of any kind can use pictures, individual words, sentence-fills, acting, and oral questions and responses as well as formal written questions.

- A questionnaire. Students answer direct questions about what they need English for. You can include questions such as "What is the hardest thing to do in English for you?" or "How often do you read instructions in English?"

- A timeline, where students indicate tasks that they need to do in English on a daily or weekly basis. The timeline could also include future tasks the student would like to be able to do in English.

- A list of activities. Students write the various tasks that they do in English, how often they have to do them, and how important the tasks are.

- An educational history. Students write where they studied English before and how well they did.

- A book survey. Have students go through the textbook and note down topics that they are interested in, activities or exercises that look interesting, and learning points that they believe will help them.

- Corner surveys. For lower-level students, you can label the corners of the room with different answers. Students answer questions by choosing a corner. For example, label the corners Reading, Writing, Listening, and Speaking. Ask students to choose the skill they need the most work on. Then ask which skill they are best at. You can also do yes or no questions by labeling sides of the classroom.

- A formal evaluation such as a speaking test or a standardized proficiency test.

---

* *The corner survey idea comes from Woodward (1994).*

After class, compile what you have learned and identify the main needs and interests of the class as a whole. Once you have a sense of the students' needs and interests, you can adapt your approach and the activities you do in class to reflect those needs and interests. Make sure to refer back to them throughout the class term, telling students, for example, "We are doing this note-taking exercise because many of you want to go to university in the United States."

Goal Setting

This form of needs evaluation is simple and motivational, as it focuses students on their goals.

1 Ask students to write down one goal they have for learning English. It might be to study at a university or to be able to travel or to do better at their job.

2 Now ask them to think of three to five specific skills they need to accomplish their goal. For example, to study at a university, you have to be able to write an essay in English, understand a lecturer, and read dense texts.

3 Now that they have clear, specific objectives, tell them to try to find people with the same objectives as them. When they meet, have them share ideas for how to achieve their goals.

4 At the end of the activity, you can collect the papers and find the most common goals and objectives to guide your teaching.

5 This activity can lead to students creating an independent study plan that they follow throughout the term.

Complete the Sentence*

Another way to survey students with open-ended questions.

1 Give students sentences to complete. Students complete the sentences to tell you about their expectations for the class or their difficulties in English. You can write these to target anything you would like to know. Some of my favorite incomplete sentences include "I like learning about...," "I learn well when I...," "I think...is hard," and" I need to do...in English."

2 You can also allow students to turn the tables on you and ask you to fill out some sentences, such as

   • "I give high grades to students who..."

   • "One way to learn English well is..."

   • "In class, I like to..."

   • "I think homework is important because..."

---

* *This idea came from Woodward (2009).*

Class Survey*

This is a way to test language and also build a sense of community.

1 Ask the class a survey-type question such as, "How many of you have finished high school?" or "How many of you live near the school?" or "How many of you like chocolate?"

2 Record the answers on the board and make a sentence about the result, such as "Most of us live near the school" or "No one likes chocolate", or have students do it. For more advanced students, you could practice percentages or comparatives with sentences such as "33% of us like chocolate" or "More students in class like strawberry ice cream than chocolate."

3 Continue doing this a few times before shifting to questions about English study, needs, or other things you want to know about them.

4 Students can also ask their own getting-to-know-you questions to the class and draw their own conclusions.

---

* *I learned about this activity in Woodward (2009).*

What Do You Know?

This is a way to find out what a class has already learned. Examples are given for lower-level students as well as higher-level classes.

1   Ask students to tell you one thing they know about English.

2   Put some ideas on the board such as

  • I know that the word for _____ in English is _____.

  • If I want to do _____, I say _____.

  • _____ is an informal way to say _____.

  • _____ tense is used to _____.

3   Have students discuss their knowledge of English. This is a great way to see what they know, what kinds of things they know, and how they categorize knowledge, and maybe even a way to dispel some myths.

Pantomime Introductions*

This is a lesson I came up with, based on the direct method, and shaped by some material on esl.about.com. *I used it with a class of absolute beginners to great success.*

1 Start by saying, "Hello!" and waving at the class. Smile. Repeat this until you get a response, hopefully something like "Hello!" back.

2 Move around the class saying hello to various students individually, eliciting hello back.

3 Now say to the class, "Hello, I am Mr. Burns," using your own name and preferred form of address. Point at yourself as you speak.

4 Go around the room, introducing yourself to students with the same sentence. Try to elicit an introduction from them.

5 Make this into a name-memorization activity by circling back to previous students so that you repeat their names several times.

6 Now add "He is" and "she is," by saying "I am Mr. Burns. He is Ali," while pointing at a student.

7 Point at various students and ask, "He is...?" After a few repetitions you can elicit the whole sentence.

8 You can make mistakes to elicit responses too. Point at George and say, "He is John?"

9 In the same way, you can cover to-be questions, "You are?" and "Who are you?"

---

*   *This activity is adapted from an idea from* esl.about.com.

Label the Classroom

This is a great way to assess and teach lots of names of things in the classroom. It's also a great thing to do with a low-level class that may not have a lot of vocabulary yet.

1 Bring a lot of sticky notes to class.

2 Ask students to name things in the classroom and then label them. Depending on the level of the student, this can be done a few ways:

   • Students write the words they know and then label the items. Other students are free to correct as they see fit.

   • You prepare labels with words and students put the labels in the correct place.

   • You tour the room, prompting students to tell you the names of things. Ask students to name it, write the name on a label, and label it. You step in to name or write any words they don't know or can't spell.

   • You can add verbs or adjectives to your survey. Next to the light switch you can add "Turn on. Turn off." On the door, you can add "Open" and "Shut" labels.

   • This can also be expanded to include the whole school. You can even turn this into an orientation by explaining the purpose of various places in the school.

Classroom English Pantomime

This is a good way to assess and teach basic classroom commands, especially chunks like "Open your book." It's compatible with the total physical response approach and the direct method. It's designed for beginning-level students, but it can be adapted to teach any classroom English you want students to know.

1 Sit down on a chair in front of the class and say, "Stand up." Then stand. If students do not stand, repeat until they do. Use hand gestures, smiles, encouragement. Make sure to repeat "Stand up" throughout. If permissible, you can pick out a student and stand them up.

2 Once the class is standing, say, "Sit down." Sit down yourself. Continue acting out and repeating "Sit down" until the class is sitting.

3 Repeat these steps several times until the whole class is comfortably standing up and sitting down upon command.

4 You can use this same procedure (give a simple command, do it yourself, pantomime, encourage the students to repeat through gestures, smiles, and tongue-clucking) to teach almost any simple command. I like to cover these:

  • Get out the book

  • Get a piece of paper

  • Get a pen/get a pencil

  • Get X from the shelf

  • Put X back on the shelf

  • Open the book/close the book

  • Write down/write your name

  • Come to the board

  • Line up

  • Go to your seat

Once you get through the basic ones, there's no reason you couldn't do "Get out a red pen," "Turn to page 23," "Highlight X words," and so on. Once students have the vocabulary down, the exercise can become a fun game or a race. You can even let students give commands.

Simon Says

Children's games are another great source of activities for the ESL/ EFL classroom, because they tend to require simple or repetitive language. Simon Says requires students to pay close attention to your words to know whether or not they are expected to do an action. Follow up Classroom English Pantomime with a game of Simon Says.

1 Explain the rules to the students. You will give commands. When you say "Simon says" before the command, the students should obey it. If you don't say "Simon says," they shouldn't obey it.

2 Demonstrate by saying "Simon says stand up." Stand up and encourage the class to stand. Now say, "Sit down," but don't sit. Remind students that you didn't say "Simon says," so they shouldn't sit.

3 Play the game, giving classroom commands such as "Open your book," "Get out a pen," "Come to the board," and so on, being sure to vary starting with "Simon says" or not. The fun part of the game is trying to trick students into acting even when you have not said "Simon says."

4 If students are comfortable with the vocabulary, one of them can give commands, too.

Mother May I?

Review classroom commands and practice forming questions with this adaptation of a classic children's game. Students should already know basic classroom commands.

1 Explain the rules to students. A student should ask, "Mother, may I ..." and then add an action that can be done in the classroom, such as, "Mother, may I put a pencil on my desk?" You then either say, "Yes, you may." Or "No, you may not." If you say no, you can then give another command such as, "You may put a marker on the desk."

2 Continue playing, varying saying Yes and No, and giving each student a chance to make a request, until the students are comfortable with the commands.

3 You can also let the students be "Mother" and take requests.

Word Association Brainstorm

This is one of my favorite activities to introduce a new theme or unit. On the first day of school, you can use it to see what students know about a topic and discover vocabulary gaps.

1 Put a word on the board. The word should be related to the vocabulary you want to assess students' knowledge of. The word might be *classroom* to see what classroom words students know, or *colors* to see what colors they know.

2 Ask students to write down the first five words that come to their mind when they think of that word.

3 Have students call out their words. As they do, write all unique words on the board. Do not censor or evaluate at this point.

4 Once you have the list on the board, you can go through the list and point out words that are clearly and strongly connected.

5 When you come to words that are unusual, you can ask for clarification. This often leads to interesting stories. It also can lead to the revelation of mistakes or misunderstandings.

6 When you come to words that do not seem correct or represent a mistake, ask the class whether they see the connection. See if you can puzzle out a correct word. In the context of a classroom, if a student says, "dining room," you might elicit "cafeteria" instead, as that is the place where people eat at a school.

7 In this way, you can assess their knowledge of vocabulary as well as gaps in their vocabulary.

Variation

You can also use this activity to elicit phrases or sentences or even short stories. This allows you to assess knowledge of grammar or useful phrases. In this case, instead of writing a theme word, write a word that can elicit the language you are looking for. For example, you could write *hotel* and elicit useful language for staying at a hotel, such as "I'd like a room for one person."

To assess grammar, use a prompt that will elicit sentences with the correct grammar. A prompt such as *vacation* could elicit the past tense as students talk about past vacations. In this variation, have students write sentences or useful phrases on the board. As a class, you can go over them and discuss their meaning as well as correct any errors.

Picture Words

Students guess words based on pictures. It's a great way to assess their vocabulary knowledge.

1 Tell students you will draw a picture on the board and they have to guess what it is. Tell them that you cannot speak while they guess; you can only draw.

2 Encourage students to shout out answers as you draw. Be sure to respond to their suggestions. For example, if you are drawing a cow and they guess horse, add an udder or horns. For more advanced students, you may need to draw related words or little situations if the word is abstract. Alternatively, you can draw clues to the sound of the word: for "teaspoon" you could draw a teabag and then a spoon.

3 Students can play the game in pairs or small groups. To make it easy, you can give them a category such as "classroom items" or "sports."

Classroom Scavenger Hunt

This is an active and fun way to review classroom objects and prepositions.

1 Prepare a series of clues, on small pieces of paper or index cards, that lead students around the classroom. The clues should lead to specific locations in the classroom. For lower-level students, these should be straightforward, such as "Look under the white bookcase." For higher-level students, they could be more complex, such as "Look under the tall furniture where we keep the things we like to read."

2 To make it more fun and also to assess knowledge of basic actions, you can add an activity students must do before finding the next clue. For example, a clue could say, "Put a red book on the teacher's desk. Then find the next clue inside the dictionary."

3 Choose one clue to be the starting clue. Place a second clue in the place the first clue indicates. Place a third clue in the place the third clue indicates, and so on. In the place of the last clue, include a prize of some kind—a small candy or pencil or a fun certificate.

4 Depending on how many students you have, you will want to prepare two or three scavenger hunts. You can do this by creating multiple copies of the same clues or by creating completely separate hunts. It is helpful to color code the clues by making one set all on blue paper and another all of yellow paper, for example.

5 Students working in teams have to follow the set of clues and find the prize at the end. You can do this as a race where the first team to finish wins, if you like.

Flashcards

Flashcards are a great way to study vocabulary or almost anything else. Use this simple flashcards game to test students' vocabulary on the first day and teach them a basic study skill.

1   Before class, prepare flashcards that have a set of vocabulary you want students to know on one side and the definitions on the other. Make one set of flashcards for each pair of students in class.

2   Put students in pairs. Give each pair a set of flashcards.

3   Have students take turns picking up a flashcard and without showing it to the other student, reading the word. The other student must say the definition.

4   Once students have gone through the deck without making more than two mistakes, have them pick up a card and read the definition while the other student guesses the word.

Sentence Auction Assessment*

Often used as a review exercise, a sentence auction can also assess what grammar or vocabulary points students already know.

1 Choose some vocabulary words or a set of grammar points that you want to assess students' knowledge of. Write ten to twenty sentences that use the vocabulary or grammar. About half of them should be incorrect. This works well when you simulate the most common errors students make. You also may want to make pairs of sentences to guide students. For example, sentence 3 can be "I enjoy skating." And sentence 4 can be "I enjoy to skate."

2 In class, tell students they have $2,000 to use to buy sentences. They can bid in multiples of $50. Remind them that since they have a limited amount of money, they can only buy a limited number of sentences. Tell them that their job is to buy correct sentences only. Their final score will be the number of correct sentences they buy minus the number of incorrect sentences they buy.

3 Put the sentences on the board or hand them out in worksheets. Don't give them time to review the sentences.

4 Run the auction. Ask students to bid on each sentence one at a time, until there is a clear high bid.. Keep track of who bought which sentence and also how much money the buyer has left. If a student runs out of money, they cannot bid anymore.

5 At the end, go over the sentences and reveal which are correct. Be sure to correct the incorrect sentences as a class.

6 For each student, add up their score by subtracting the number of incorrect sentences from the number of correct sentences they bought. The student with the highest score wins. If two students have the same score, the student with the most money left wins.

---

* *I first read about this activity on Dave's ESL Café (*www.eslcafe.com*).*

I Am a Word

While this activity can be used to teach grammar points, it can also be used on the first day of school to see what students know about word order, verb tense, or parts of speech.

1   Choose a grammar point you want to evaluate. Grammar that works well with this activity includes word order, verb tenses, gerund vs. infinitive, and prepositions—anything where students have to decide on the order of words and which words are included or not included.

2   Write a sentence that uses that grammar point, one that it is easy to substitute different words into. For example, if you want to test modal verbs, you could make a sentence such as "You should wear socks." It's easy to substitute many words for *you* (*I, he, she, the doctor*), should (*can, must, ought to*), and socks (*a shirt, pants, a scarf*).

3   Write the words of the sentence on large cards or sheets of paper, one word per card, large enough to be seen from the whole classroom. Then add cards for variations in the sentence. Be sure to think of how changing the sentence might involve changing other words. For the modal verb example, you'll want to include a card for *to* because some modal verbs require the word *to* (*have to, ought to*). If you are evaluating verb tense, be sure you have verbs in different tenses.

4   Put the cards on a table in front of the class. Guide students to form the original sentence by standing in a line, holding the cards.

5   Have a student swap with one of the original students. For the modal example, tell the student holding *should* to step down. Get another student to hold *have*.

6   Ask students if the sentence is correct. Encourage someone to correct it. In this example, they would correct it by grabbing the card *to* and standing between *have* and *wear*.

7 Continue swapping words in and out, checking whether the sentence is correct. If it is incorrect, let students try to correct it. This might involve changing word order, adding words, or taking out words.

8 Continue until you feel you have a grasp on their understanding of the target grammar.

Dry Run

In classes where students are learning English for a particular situation, such as making business presentations or checking in at an airport, a great way to assess what they can and can't do is to make them do it. It's also a great way to show the students what they are good at and what they need to work at.

1 Think of a task that your students should be able to do when they have completed your course. Obviously, it will need to be something that they can do in class in a limited amount of time. Reading and taking notes on a novel will not work, but reading and presenting on a short article could. Interactive group activities such as a role play tend to work best.

   Sample tasks include checking in to a hotel or at the airport, going to a restaurant, writing a business memo, giving a brief presentation, asking a friend for advice, and leading a discussion on a specific topic.

2 Choose a student or group of students who seem confident and easygoing. Make sure that they understand that the goal of the exercises is to see what they can do and that you do not expect them to succeed.

3 Ask the students to act out the task. Do not allow them to be frustrated, but do not step in to help them too soon. Take copious notes of what is good and bad.

4 When they come to a logical end or are clearly stuck, stop the students. You may then want to have other students or groups try the activity, or you may want to move to a related activity.

Setting the Tone

Rule-Breaking Role Play

This is a classic introduction-to-the-rules activity, often done at a first-day-of-school assembly. However, in class it can be much more effective, as students can reflect on the rules that were broken and why they are important.

Teacher Centered

You as the teacher (possibly with an assistant) act out the worst student you can imagine. There are a few ways to do it:

- Make a skit. Ask a fellow teacher or a student to pretend to be a teacher. Then interrupt the "teacher," talk on your cell phone, lose your homework, ask questions without listening, and do anything else that you *don't* want students to do. Then come out of character and list everything you did wrong. This is a good time to take what-if questions, such as "What if my phone rings and it's an emergency?" and "What if I really did forget to do my homework?"

  Hamming it up too much is tempting, but if you make it too entertaining, students might not relate to your character. So try to keep it within the bounds of realistic behavior. Also be sure students are aware that you are deliberately modeling bad behavior, as you might create a bad impression on the first day and undermine your authority as a teacher.

- Insert bad behavior into the first lesson surreptitiously. Ask a student a question. As they start to speak, pull out your phone and start visibly reacting to it. Let students start laughing, or cue them that you are being deliberately bad. Discuss what you did wrong, and write down the rule: "No cellphones in class" (or "Listen to each other").

  Next, tell students you have an important handout for them, and then fail to find it. Tell them that you forgot to do your work last night because there was a great TV show on and you got distracted.

Ask them whether that's ok. Again, write down the rule, "Be prepared for class."

Continue in this vein until you've written down all the rules you wanted students to follow. As in the activity above, make sure it's clear that you are modeling bad behavior on purpose.

Student Centered

Students tend to know what they should and shouldn't do in the classroom. Letting students act out the part of a bad student helps them internalize the rules and the reasoning behind them. It also allows them to argue about rules that they think are arbitrary.

- Instead of you breaking the rules, ask students to play bad students. By giving them the chance to do the wrong thing, you'll raise their awareness of what they should be doing.

- Ask students to role-play a classroom. Especially if your students are from another country or culture, this is a great chance to see what kind of rules and classroom behavior they are used to. In this case, you may want to have students start with a well-behaved class and then get them to demonstrate rules that get broken.

Classroom Rules Negotiation

Research and experience show students are more likely to follow rules if they are a part of the decision-making process. And getting them to suggest rules gives you an idea of what they think a classroom should look like.

1 Put students in pairs or small groups.

2 Have them make a T-chart on a piece of paper. Have them label one column *should* and another column *shouldn't*.

3 Tell them to think of three rules for each side, that is, three things they can do in the classroom and three things they cannot do. You could also adapt this to make it *can* and *can't*, where *can* stands for good habits and *can't* stands for rules.

4 Make a big T-chart on the board. Have each group write their rules on the board, skipping any rules that have already been written down. Alternatively, collect the rules yourself and compile them yourself.

5 If there are a lot of rules or a lot of rules that seem unnecessary or inappropriate, you could start a class discussion on the reasoning behind each rule and then a class vote on each rule. Final rules should be written up on a nice poster.

6 Another alternative is to have students vote on consequences. Ask them, "What should we do if someone ...?" completing the question with "talks on their cellphone" or "doesn't do their homework," for example. You should have some say here, but let students give some thought to what the appropriate consequences should be. This helps them think about why certain activities are not allowed and also makes them more accepting of the punishment.

Routine Modeling

This works particularly well with younger children and classrooms that have many transitions throughout the day, but it can also be used with students with lower levels of English and students who are new to the classroom.

1   Pick a routine that you want students to follow. It might be how to ask to be excused from the room or the test-taking routine or doing literary stations.

2   Ask to borrow a student's desk. Sit down and pretend to be a student. Then go through all of the steps that you want students to do in the routine. This may require you to enlist a student as a teacher and give them directions on what to say. In general, minimize talking and do your best to act out the routine. Don't forget all the details, and don't break character.

3   When you are finished, you can ask the students to act it out with you or ask targeted questions to ensure comprehension.

Study Habits Myths

It's a popular way to start a lecture, so why not start your class by polling the class and then debunking any myths?

1   Write down a list of three to five pieces of advice you want to pass on to students about learning and studying.

2   Think of three to five common myths about studying that you wish to dispel.

3   Make a list of all the statements from steps 1 and 2 in which you mix up the advice and myths in random order.

4   Present the list to the class on the board, on a projector, or on a worksheet. Ask students to say which statements are true and which are false.

5   Reveal the answers and go over them with students, giving them an idea of best ways to study.

Sharing Tips

Have students teach each other how to study well.

1 Put students in pairs. Ask them to share one piece of advice for learning English with one another.

2 Alternatively, have each pair agree on five pieces of advice. Then as a class you can whittle the list down to the top ten pieces of advice.

3 You can also give each pair a particular area of English. Pair 1 talks about how to learn vocabulary. Pair 2 talks about how to learn grammar. Pair 3 talks about how to practice speaking, and so on.

4 Students can wrap up by writing their advice on posters to hang around the class.

Syllabus Scavenger Hunt

If you have a student handbook or syllabus, instead of reading it to students, have them search it for the rules.

1   Prepare a worksheet with either questions or cloze statements that students can answer from the syllabus or student handbook. Statements might include "What are the only reasons I can have an excused absence from class?" or "The final exam is worth ___% of my grade."

2   Hand out the syllabus or rulebook and the worksheet. Have students fill in the worksheet, thus learning the rules for your class.

3   Go over the answers to be sure they are correct and to address any questions or concerns.

Variation

You can also give each student one question to search for. As you go over the answers, you can ask each student to give their answer.

If you prefer giving a lecture at the beginning of class on the rules, make a handout as described above that students can use as a note-taking device. Since you provide the questions, you can be sure they will stay on track. Taking notes helps them internalize the information.

References

Orange County Department of Education. (2011, June 20). Ice breakers and name games. Retrieved from www.ocde.us/AVID /Documents/icebreakers.pdf.

Ur, P. (1988). Grammar practice activities: A practical guide for teachers. Cambridge, U.K.: Cambridge University Press.

Ur, P. & Wright, A. (1992). Five-minute activities: A resource book of short activities. Cambridge, U.K.: Cambridge University Press.

Woodward, T. (2009). Planning lessons and courses: Designing sequences of work for the language classroom (11th ed.). Cambridge, U.K.: Cambridge University Press.

51298857R00041

Made in the USA
San Bernardino, CA
18 July 2017